Praise for *The Sky Watc*

"*The Sky Watched* bears witness to Native experience. In Linda LeGarde Grover's work, time runs backward through Ojibwe creation myths and explanation tales to find strength for the later years of boarding school and all the upheavals of the new world. Family plays a major role as does the roundness of moon, owl nest, gratitude, and the 'grace of this merciful earth.' There is heaven and hell in these heavenly poems."

—Diane Glancy, author of *Pushing the Bear*

"Linda LeGarde Grover's *The Sky Watched* is a beautiful litany of poems about Anishinaabe lives. She weaves English and Anishinaabemowin in lovely and innovative ways, and what is left at the end of the collection is a heartbreaking symphony full of many voices, all coming together with their own sorrowing but merciful hands."

—Erika Wurth, author of *Crazy Horse's Girlfriend*

"This is the first bilingual poetry book in English/Ojibwe: not translations, but poems using both languages. Linda LeGarde Grover's *The Sky Watched* is a poetic reaction, in a wonderfully realistic voice, of spirit and essence of the Ojibwe people. Read it and be transformed, as readers of *Beowulf* and El Cid and other national epics have been throughout the ages."

—Geary Hobson, author of *Plain of Jars*

"*The Sky Watched* is a book of and for community. It is a book of witness. It testifies to survivance as, according to its last lines, 'a continuing song / since long before the memory of mortals.'"

—*Kenyon Review*

"Remember, remember, remember, Linda LeGarde Grover's wonderful book demands. And she does. Again and again. Old tales from the Ojibwe tradition and new stories from mission schools and relocations where 'a tangle of children smell home in their dreams.' She captures the taste of recipes and the feel of beading bracelets alongside injustices minor as a navy bean and major as a lost language. These are poems as sad and essential as a field of cotton flowers. You will remember them."

—Jeffrey Thompson, author of
Birdwatching in Wartime and *Fragile*

"Linda LeGarde Grover tells of a calico flowered beanbag that when 'split it spilled the past,' just as her poems spill extraordinary perceptions infused with Ojibwe spirituality along with haunting insight of raw boarding school memories that house a continent of pain and despair. *The Sky Watched* is an intuitive voice of reverence that understands the power of the spirit."

—Denise Lajimodiere, author of *Stringing Rosaries*

"Her formal innovation is to include poems written partly or completely in Ojibwe. In a collection about the systematic eradication of Indian language, this subtly tells a powerful story about resistance and survival."

—*Star Tribune*

The Sky Watched

Also by Linda LeGarde Grover
Published by the University of Minnesota Press

Gichigami Hearts: Stories and Histories from Misaabekong

Onigamiising: Seasons of an Ojibwe Year

The Road Back to Sweetgrass

In the Night of Memory

The Sky Watched

Poems of Ojibwe Lives

Linda LeGarde Grover

UNIVERSITY OF MINNESOTA PRESS

MINNEAPOLIS

LONDON

The Publication History on pages 111–13 gives original and previous publication history for the writings compiled in this book.

First published in 2016 by Red Mountain Press

First University of Minnesota Press edition, 2022

Published by the University of Minnesota Press
111 Third Avenue South, Suite 290
Minneapolis, MN 55401–2520
http://www.upress.umn.edu

ISBN 978-1-5179-1451-6 (pb)

Library of Congress record available at https://lccn.loc.gov/2022015044.

Printed in the United States of America on acid-free paper

The University of Minnesota is an equal-opportunity educator and employer.

30 29 28 27 26 25 24 23 22   10 9 8 7 6 5 4 3 2 1

To my daughters Waaboosoons, Giizis, and Waawaashkeshii
and to my sister Susie

Winters she became the sun; summers, the moon.

Contents

III. Anishinaabewi

IV. Gichi-Anishinaabewi

Preface

This edition of *The Sky Watched,* which was first published by Red Mountain Press in 2016, is a revised and expanded collective memoir in poetry of Anishinaabe/Ojibwe people of the western Great Lakes regions. The poems include spiritual teachings, experiences of individuals ages ago and yesterday, the impact of European and American settler cultures on traditions and religious practices as well as the lives of individuals, families, communities, and tribes. Interwoven throughout, I hope, is that uniquely Ojibwe way of looking at the world in the context of walking the road of Bimaa-diziwin, the living of a good life. Ojibwewag walking that road meet all they encounter with those values that have been handed down from generation to generation: humility, gratitude, generosity, and an awareness of the world around us.

The Sky Watched is organized into four parts, in acknowl-edgment of the time-honored significance of the number four in Ojibwe tradition and belief. The pattern is evident and constant in our lives: there are four directions, four sacred colors, four seasons. There are four sacred medicines (tobacco, cedar, sweetgrass, and sage) that are the grandmothers of all the other medicines. The four parts of *The Sky Watched* follow the four human ages, inter-twined with the ages of the Earth: Oshkabinoojiinh awi, Abinoojiinh awi, Anishinaabewi, and Gichi-Anishinaabewi (infancy, childhood, adulthood, elderhood).

Part I, Oshkabinoojiinh awi, introduces Daadibaajimoowinini, the storyteller manifest in a turtle sculpture by Gordon Van Wert, who guides us into poems about Ojibwe histories and spirits, es-tablishing a worldview that will be damaged but not destroyed. In Part II, Abinoojiinh awi, poems speak of the impacts of the Indian boarding school era on Ojibwe lives, individual and collective, and on the destruction of practices and relationships that had held the world together for generations. The poems in Part III, Anishi-naabewi, interpret life after the end of boarding schools—the picking up of pieces, the searching for lost pieces, and the hopeful but realistic endeavors to survive and continue in the midst of tremendous loss. Part IV, Gichi-Anishinaabewi, addresses contemporary issues that are linked to both the beauty of the teachings in Part I and the destructions and means of survival in Parts II and III.

One of the threads running through and connecting all four parts is the consideration of what it means to be Anishinaabe: what did it mean in earlier times, and how have those foundational beliefs morphed, and morphed again, seeming to change and shift shape yet always returning to Debwewin, the truth.

I

Oshkabinoojiinh awi

Dadibaajimoowinini, the Storyteller

To the sculpture by Gordon Van Wert, Red Lake Nation,
at the University of Minnesota Duluth Tweed Museum of Art

———

The color of gabbro in thick greenery he takes the form of a turtle,
this wise and compassionate healer
honored with the weight of knowledge, leaning heavily on a stick,
he bears on his back a circle of red,
petroglyph symbols,
of ancient wisdoms that will be revealed
at the time planned by the Creator.

Dadibaajimoowinini, the storyteller
who is also Gitigaaninini the gardener,
tends the stories,
the foundation of our existence as a people
and of our place in the corporal and spiritual worlds
and as planned by the Creator.
At those times, seasons that have always
since before time existed were meant to be,
he speaks from the lush and living greenery
where the stories, tended, have bloomed.
Dadibaajimoowinini the storyteller
who is also Gitigaaninini the gardener
speaks; we, who have waited with patience
hear the stories; listening we ponder,
honored to accept and bear their weight.
Together, then, storyteller and students
weave the knowledge that passes
generation to generation into the fabric
of our stories and existence,
the spirits of all that has been
and what will come to be.

Redemption

Long before the memory of mortals a bitter feud between Nanaboozhoo and the Mishibizhiig, the spirits of the lake, led to a Great Flood that covered the Earth. Nanaboozhoo and four animals who survived floated on a raft of driftwood looking for a surface upon which they could live and walk. Amik (Beaver), Ojig (Fisher), and Nigiig (Otter) each exhausted their strengths diving to find ground beneath the floodwater, but they were unable to stay underwater long enough to find the bottom. As they despaired, the smallest animal, Wazhashk (Muskrat), asked to take a turn. Nanaboozhoo and the others told him that it was hopeless and not to try, but the muskrat insisted. It is because of the courage and sacrifice of Wazhashk that the Earth was renewed.

Wazhashk, the sky watched this.
Mewinzhaa, long before the memory of mortals
Wazhashk, the sky watched your timid, gallant warrior body
    deliberate and then dive, plunging
    with odd grace and dreadful fragility
    into translucent black water,
    dark mystery unknown and fast as the night sky
and barely—to a single inhalation shared by a weeping four
and a hopeful splash quieter than an oar—break the surface
    into concentric expanding disappearing rings as
    water circled your departure,
    for a moment transparently covering
    rose-gray soles small seed pearl toes
    above your determined small warrior body
    that hurtled from sight,
    in an instant pulled into cold dark depths,
seeking the finite in the veins of a waterlocked Earth.

Wazhashk, the water covering the Earth watched.
Mewinzhaa, long before the memory of mortals
Wazhashk, when you were obscured from the sky
the water watched you
    lost from the sight of the praying four
    crouched on the small raft afloat on vast water
grown faint under crushing cold
    alone then below the waterline
    seeking the finite in the veins of a cumbrous earth,
    waterfingers intruding invading
    all unguarded aspects of your small warrior body
    now stiff and graceless, pulled by will
    into icy dark depths.

Wazhashk, in that dark mystery
unknown and vast as the night sky
you continued your solitary plunge
    lost from the sight of all who lived above water,
    who considered your size and your courage,
until in cold and exhaustion your silent voice whispered
    ningosh nindakamj
    nindayekoz niwiinibaa
    I am tired I must sleep
and was heard by the Great Spirit.

Wazhashk, you were heard and were answered
    mangide'en, anamiindim mangide'en
    gaawin gimbezhigo siin
    anamiindim mangide'en
    have courage, have courage in the depths
    you are not alone
    have courage, have courage in the depths
till your spirit rose and spoke
    geget geget
    through my despair I will

and the Great Spirit watched this and guided you.
Mewinzhaa, long before the memory of mortals,
Wazhashk, the Great Spirit guided you and watched
	your small curled brown fingers
	stretch their curving pink-nailed claws
	to grasp the muddy, rocky breast
	of a waiting Mother Earth.

And today, Wazhashk, hear us breathe,
inhaling and exhaling a continuing song
of your courage and sacrifice, your grace
our redemption a continuing song
since long before the memory of mortals.

With each telling of the story, with each singing of the song
we once again rise to break the surface seeking then finding
the finite beyond the grace of this merciful Earth
the finite beyond the mercy of this graceful Earth.

Oshkabinoojiinh awi

Kwesens Conceives Nanaboozhoo

*Mewinzhaa, a long time ago, before she became Nokomis,
grandmother of Nanaboozhoo, the moon's most beloved
daughter was envied by her sisters the stars, who tricked her
into falling to Earth from their home, the sky. She gave birth to
a daughter, Kwesens, whom she sheltered carefully, wanting to
protect her from all harm and danger; however, Kwesens strayed
from her mother while they were out digging potatoes from their
small garden site. She was swept into a violent whirlwind in a
dark storm caused by the North Wind and became pregnant.
Nokomis, who grieved terribly when her daughter died in
childbirth, raised her grandson Nanaboozhoo with patience and
wisdom, remembering and honoring Kwesens.*

Trees whistle a warning and look to the sky
as shivering blue stones dance in liquid blue field
and listening moccasins warily step
soft up, soft up and a turn, the freeze
as the North Wind seizes the night.

An ice snake winds past Old Woman Moon
his cloudless stealth feinting gusts of breath
and shocked stars rue their jealous past
watching First Daughter spin on the edge of the world
as the North Wind takes the night.

Windigo Bimose

At the end of that last summer
    that last summer we were like you
    so dry it was, and so hot
when even the pines could give us no shade
and their brown, sharp needles, paler each day, fell
    at first I thought the sound was rain
in drifts beneath dying branches
where they cut and scratched our feet till they swelled

then at the time of day that no shadows were cast
a piece of fire fell from the sky
and the sun grew on the ground.
Ravenous, it began to eat the earth.

Carrying babies, grandparents, the infirm
we fled, for a time ahead of the smoke and flames
but after the barren hungry summer
we were in a weakened state, even
the strongest. One by one we made the choice
to continue alone or die with our families;
    I cannot fault one's decision to stay
    or another's to abandon
for myself, after my old parents, my wife
and our children all but one fell like pine needles.
I chose to walk with my firstborn.

My oldest daughter who'd always been
strong as a man and slow to tire
walked beside me for how long
    days, nights, lifetimes.
When she tripped and fell, the others
    by then fewer in number
    than the fingers on both my hands

        Oshkabinoojiinh awi

watched without hope or interest
would I have done the same if I were them
her struggle to stand, singed lids closing
slowly slowly over dull desiccated eyes.

I lifted her, my firstborn. My heart recalled
        her birth, her mother
        her small brothers and sisters
        her grandparents
and tore. Rent, it spilled and emptied.

Then from emptiness great hunger emerged
        much like had the sun's in summer
and through the air
        less smoky now, and cold
sensing from the north a corporal warmth
        a young mother's arms and breast
and a sound from the north, a lost child's cry
        young bones and skin tender
        ice-cut feet bleeding into snow

Follow me; let us walk, I said to the others.

Ravenous, I lifted my daughter.
Ravenous, I carried her across my shoulders.
Ravenous, I stepped the first step
        follow me, let us walk
and then ravenous, the remnant rose and followed.

We had fled from heat to seek the cold,
endless cold our dark and everlasting life
where we never slept again, and where
in endless appetite we search for you
        your warm breath
        your blood that flows bright
        and steams in winter air.

Oshkabinoojiinh awi   9

How we despise your frailties, envy your souls,
how we love and hate your living flesh;
how we yearn and crave past death
past life we hunger, and we walk today.

Sea Smoke on Gichigami

Little Spirit Moon, Great Spirit Moon,
Bear Moon, and Snow Crust Moon
   the four moons of winter

Sunrise
   these coldest mornings of gelid moons
searing the horizon, slicing dawn from night
red-orange light captured on facets of ice crystals
that spin and glitter in the air, falling
to the caul of translucent marble
that covers Gichigami.

Beneath that frozen vastness
the lake world stirs with the earth
  light diffused to the palest of golds
  rouses spirits curled in sleep
    on the valleyed lake floor; awake
    they push with scaled claws and rise
      these coldest mornings of gelid moons
their breath a song to the world above the ice

delicate inhalations
from the sliver of space between ice and lake
expel to white steam, sea smoke a silver mist
rising in vapor columns over the surface of the lake.

On the shore an old man lifts a hand
    to the morning; the wind lifts tobacco from his palm,
    scattering the offering in four directions
watching the song
gray white silver
drifting rolling across ice.

The song begins with spring
and the Creator who made the earth
        streams rivers lakes oceans
        grass plants flowers trees
          the medicines the seasons
        birds animals insects
and finally the first man,
born to the granddaughter of the moon.

Shimmering cold in summers of the past
the lake carried them weightless buoyant floating
    sun glinting on wet scales and claws
      on the shore they rested
      against gabbrous rock heated by the sun,
this before rancor reached the world
before the Great Flood and finally redemption
    and the retreat to the underwater,
    the cold darkness of the valley a grace of sorts.

Since then, in early autumn
when skies reflect gentian waters of the lake
    spirits rise with the tide, lured
    by the colors of the hillside
    water-blurred red orange yellow leaves
    against the black of rocky cliffs
yet obliquely they gaze, cautiously
remembering the spirit who dazzled by the brilliance
drifted lost toward an inlet
where a young woman rowing alone
in a green-painted wooden boat
recoiled, her hair whitening.

Late-autumn ice forms and breaks
heavy on the surface of the lake
slowing the movements of the spirits

whose scales and claws
    gray and dull starving for the sun
reach above Gichigami to grasp the wind
and on the shore waves collide
      with rocks, trees
      and fragilities built by man.

In winter, cold subdues the water surface;
nights, white ice reflects the winter moons
Little Spirit Moon, Great Spirit Moon,
Bear Moon, Snow Crust Moon
in their slow sail through the sky.

Sunrise sears the horizon,
slicing dawn from night
red-orange light captured on facets of ice crystals
that spin and glitter in the air, falling
to the caul of translucent marble ice
that covers Gichigami
descending to the valleyed lake floor,
rousing the spirits curled in sleep;
awakened they push with scaled claws
    ascending toward the sun
      these coldest mornings of gelid moons.
As one, then another, and others emerge
steam rises, fog glitters in the light
their breath a silver song
to the world above the ice.

Anjeniwag, the Angels

Upon hearing Mendelssohn's *Elijah,* Op. 70
O thou, who makes thine angels spirits
performed by the Duluth Superior Symphony Orchestra

———————

This November evening
with sky purple starless
and dark yet a month away
from the longest of this year
anticipated holiness of music
lights the spirits of some
whose souls warmer than the sidewalk
melt ice crystals to footprints,
wet tracks on concrete;
the rest, pilgrims hurry inside
round-shouldered against the chill,
unwrapped cough drops in pockets
against folded bills for wine and a tip
at intermission.

Seated musicians in black wonder
what angels might bring Elijah tonight
to lovers of music, light, warmth,
Jehovah, intermission wine
served in stemless plastic
or all of these?

The conductor bows, turns
to face chorus and orchestra
the stiffness of his straight back
flexing to an arabesque,
his wingspan of raised arms;

with the swell of the oratorio,
the expectant the hopeful
the jaded the surprised
are tethered, the source
of the Aylmeri jess
invisible and tangible as
with an intake of breath
of breath, all
singers musicians
expectant hopeful jaded
transform with the opus
returning briefly to what we once were
and will be again,
anjeniwag, angels,
spirits in soul and form.

This is human-produced sound, tangible
touch of bow to string, of mouth to reed
or nickel mouthpiece, of breath to vocal chord
that calls forth Elijah;
our quickened souls
that make the music, conduct, and hear,
fly as angels over the sound
fly as anjeniwag above the sound.

II

Abinoojiinh awi

Everything You Need to Know in Life You'll Learn at Boarding School

Speak English. Forget the language of your grandparents. It is dead. Forget their teachings. They are ignorant and ungodly. Cleanliness is next to Godliness. Indians are not clean. Your mother did not teach you to be clean. Stand in line. You will learn cleanliness. This is a toothbrush. Hang it on the hook next to the others. Do not allow the bristles to touch. This spreads the disease that you bring to school from your families. Make your bed with mitered corners.

A bed not properly made will be torn apart. Start over. Remember and be grateful that the boarding school clothes and feeds you. Say grace before meals. In English. Do not cry. Crying never solved anything.

Write home once each month. In English.

Tell your mother that you are doing very well. You'll never amount to anything. Answer when the teacher addresses you. In English. We discourage visits from your family. If you visit your family in the summer, report to the matron's office immediately upon your return. You will be allowed into the dormitory after you have been sanitized and deloused. Busy hands are happy hands. Keep yourself occupied. You'll never amount to anything. Books are our friends. Reading is your key to the world. In English. Forget the language of your grandparents. It is dead. If you are heard speaking it, you will kneel on a navy bean for one hour. Do not cry. Crying never solved anything. We will ask if you have learned your lesson. You will answer. In English. Spare the rod and spoil the child. We will not spare the rod. We will cut your hair. We will shame you. We will lock you in the basement. Learn from that. Improve yourself. Speak English. Forget the language of your grandparents. It is dead. You'll never amount to anything.

The Story of Elias and Victoria, His True Love

Mewinzhaa, ninokomis gaye nimishomis gii-abinoojiwag.
Long ago, my grandmother and grandfather were children.

Ninokomis gi-zhinikaazo Victoria Muh-Quay-Mud.
Ogii-odabitoon Onamanii zaga-iganing.
My grandmother was called Victoria Muh-Quay-Mud.
She lived at Lake Vermilion.

Imishoomis gii-zhinikaazo Elias LeGarde.
Ogii-odabiitoon Nah-Gah-Chi-Wa-Nong.
My grandfather was called Elias LeGarde.
He lived at Fond du Lac.

Apii Elias gaye Victoria gi-aginoojiyiwaad,
Anishinaabe wi-abinoogiwag gii-maagiinaawag widi
gikinoo'amaading Zhaaganaashii wigawigong waasa.
When Elias and Victoria were children,
Anishinaabe children were sent away
from their homes to English school.

Elias gaye Victoria oshiimeyiwaan gii-maagiiwanag iwidi
Vermilion gikin-amaading wigamigong.
Elias and Victoria and their brothers and sisters
went away to the Vermilion boarding school.

Apii gii-maajaawaad gii-gigashkendamong gakina awiya.
Abinoojiwas gii-mawiwag.
When they left, everyone was sad.
The children cried.

Elias ogii-zaagi'aan Victoria,
minawaa Victoria obii-zaagi'aan Elias.
Elias loved Victoria,
and Victoria loved Elias.

Apii Elias gaye Victoria giigizhigiiwad, gii wiidigewag
gii-izhaawag Onigamiising.
When Elias and Victoria grew up, they got married.
They went to Duluth.

Noongoom, LeGardes odoobiitanawaa Onigamiising.
noongoom ingiw LeGarde abinoojiwag aanawa endaawaad.
Gikinoo'imawaawag amaadii wigamong Onigamiising imaa.
Noongoom LeGardes maamawi-ayaawag.

Minwendaanawaa dash.
Today the LeGardes live in Duluth.
Today the LeGarde children live at home.
They go to school in Duluth.
Today the LeGardes all live together.
And they are happy.

LeGardes omisawendaanawaa maamawi apane ji-ayaawaad.
The LeGardes will stay together forever.

Onishishin.
That is pretty (good).

South Dakota Mission School, 1890

At mission school so far away from home
at night I heard the song through dreams of trees,
birches and jack pines in rocky woods
that I walked in my white nightgown, peering
through night fog for my mother, who perhaps
might walk in her own dreams, looking for me.

Days inside the classroom, prim and chaste
we kept our dark wool dresses smooth and clean,
covered by starched white aprons bleached
immaculate by our absence of sin
and practiced English by living it,
our lives limited as our proficiency
in that language, and our peculiar use of it.

Evenings, Sister Joseph read aloud,
her pale and unlined faced benign behind
spectacles that mirrored twin gaslights
while Sister Agnes taught us fancy work,
and so we improved our English by listening,
and our skills as ladies by embroidering
handkerchiefs and petticoat hems.

Nights, across the plain we heard them sing,
the foreign Indians, throughout that icy fall.
As winter started, still the people sang
in a language that we didn't understand.
Sister Joseph said to pray for their poor souls,
those Sioux hadn't been blessed with mission school
yet, and didn't speak English.
You'll never be White if you don't try, she said;
I will confess I half-believed I could.
We mission girls had left our pagan ways

behind when we learned how to read and write
and about Jesus, and the sin of our old ways.
We tried to be like his Blessed Mother,
or as close as Christian Chippewa girls could get.
No wicked willfulness here. We had learned
to do as we were told,

which on that winter night we did, although
we didn't understand why, awakened
from righteous virgin sleeps to stand shivering
beside our narrow white iron beds
by Sister Agnes, who told us to hurry.
Wrapped in blankets pulled from off the beds
and naked under our white nightgowns
a sight to scandalize the Blessed Mother
we did as we were told,
no wicked willfulness here,
and followed Sister outside into the night
stepping across dead grass, dry and brittle
that cracked under our bare cold feet
to lie in a frozen ditch. Beneath our warmth
sparkling frost patterns on dark earth
melted, turning ice crystals to mud
that smeared shocking stains on our nightgowns
as we did as we were told.
No wicked willfulness here.

From the ravine we heard gunshots, then a keening
that rose so quickly, a sliver of smoke into the sky
and Sister said to lie still, girls, head down
and she whispered to the Blessed Mother
"Please, ask your Son to spare these baptized girls"
who did as they were told.

And what did I think, while
pressed indecently to that frozen muddy ground
as the nightgown of the girl next to me
blew skyward in the icy wind
doing its own ghost dance; did I ask why?
Did I ask for the Blessed Mother's help
and for Jesus to spare the baptized Indians?
Well, I prayed for my mother and my brother Louis.
    I prayed to see them again.
    I prayed for the other girls and for the Sisters,
    for myself, I confess; forgive me
    and for those foreign Indians the Sioux, God help them
    for mercy for us all
and then
I prayed in my own language,
my lips open and moving to release no sound
unbound silent words a visible cloud
above ice crystals melting on frozen earth
turning to mud against my body, those words
shades of blue and gray without sound those words
uncoiling winding silent cold
and as determined as the wind.

Leaving

Old enough to walk to the depot ourselves,
we waved to Ma
and she smiled back from the porch, waving
    goodbye! see you in the summer!
    take care of your little sister!
in one breath looking smaller, in another out of sight.

Turning the corner I looked back; I saw
Ma wiping her eyes on her sleeve,
coarse twilled cotton comfort
drying my tears also, I almost thought,
but it was just the wind blowing cold tracks
that dried to a salty soreness
from the corners of my eyes to my ears
as I blinked in the bright cold sun.

Brud the oldest lifted Angeline the youngest
wrapped in her new coat a warm brown
    cut down from her own
      by Ma, for starting school.

It wasn't easy. On the train
Angeline cried herself a hundred miles,
her tears a spring of misery deep as China
while our own dripped down our throats
to our stomachs, sour puddles
that in briny darkness would never dry.

Later, Angeline slept
lulled by the rumble of the train
dulled by the lullaby of grief
her face hot and thin cheeks shiny
from salty runoff, in her dreams

gasping arrhythmic short intakes of breath
that kept me awake. I looked out the window
at the progression of small towns, a movie run backwards
from our trip home last June,
and when it got too dark to see outside
I stayed turned to the window, watching
that familiar reversal of heart's order
reel after reel, children ghostly in the glass
in rehearsal it seemed for our destination,
that life backwards from all we knew at home,
Angeline Biik Mitchell and Waboos
sleeping in the glare of the overhead light
a tangle of children smelling home in dreams
as their heads rested on Ma's cut-down coat,
then my own staring face blank, tearless
smooth as stone, reflected in the window
reversed too in the glass and in my senses
in rehearsal it seemed for our destination,
that life backwards from all we knew at home.

> *left hand to right daylight to darkness*
> *yes ma'am yes sir raise your head*
> *stand at attention take your beating*
> *remember remember remember*

Ma at Home

After they turned the corner, that huddle of children
carrying bread to eat on the train, my children
with their dark coats still faces resigned feet
that had walked down the porch stairs
moving, moving, a catch of breath seen and felt

walking forward and away, a catch and a pause
but then forward, forward to the corner
in one breath looking smaller, in another out of sight

> goodbye! see you in the summer!
> take care of your little sister!

I lowered my arm and placed into its crook my smile
and my tears, the full-blown bloom of my heart
damp on a dark cotton dress sleeve.

Back in the house my hands did their tasks
without the summer help of my heart
whose seasons had changed in two beats:
picked up the quilts from the floor, folding
    gray and black wool, old skirts and trousers
    bits of red, a man's wool shirt
    faded maroon and brown, my wedding quilt
    and the lightest a summer dress, flowers blurred in fog
tucking batting where patches frayed and threads broke
    smoothing soothing mothering
    the prints of my children's bodies
to squares that I placed under the bed, until spring.
Then I walked to work, warm without my coat,
cut down for Angeline, the smallest and today the warmest
walking to the train in her huddle of brothers
in my cut-down coat, my arms around her arms

my shoulders on her shoulders
my cut-down coat warming her in my absence
my smile and wave the last she saw
my starving eyes the last she felt,
on the back of her small head the combed-in line
that parted her hair between her tiny braids.

Small Angeline.
With her brothers she walked, without them I waited,
back to my hangnail existence, three seasons deadened,
but living for the day they would return.

Bemidji

When I tucked my feet under the bench
and looked down, my legs ended at the knees,
no brown high-top shoes, no black wool stockings,
just legs that ended where my knee pants ended.
If I pushed my stomach out to a hard air-filled paunch
my hunger ended at my ribs,
no emptiness no growl no sorrow,
just an ache in the hollow of nothing to eat.

Passing time we were, my brothers and me
waiting at the bus depot for the priest
who would take us to school.
Strangers in a strange land we sat
straight and quiet as if he watched us
while we waited for him. Waited.

Lethargic homesick patient heartsick
fatigued by the wait and restless,
swinging our feet from the bench, getting up
roaming the block begging bread from a bakery
eating on the sidewalk, watching and waiting
for the priest in his black car. It's funny
nobody noticed us but the ticket seller
who ignored us and went home
leaving us to sleep there in the waiting room
on wooden benches slippery as church pews.

Awake in the dark depot that first night
I sat up, then knelt on the seat of the bench,
my mouth resting on the curved back, tasting
and smelling church, sour smell and salt
damp change, soft bills, chewing gum, matchbooks
a tackiness from other people's hands on my lips

as I passed time awake in the dark depot, waiting
for the priest in his black car. It's funny
nobody noticed us, nobody missed us.

The baker lady fed us twice, children like
cautious squirrels or timid fledglings
small-town wildlife nearly tamed,
carrying that leftover bread back
past the eyes of the passive ticket seller
to our den our nest our chapel the depot
our new life, that brick and concrete waiting room
a purgatory between home and boarding school.

Then that second morning, uneasy though we were
the dread of returning to Indian school lessened
ever so slightly and we began to hope, maybe
we would shine shoes, wash dishes
find lost change on the sidewalk
and we'd buy tickets home from the ticket seller
who wouldn't say, Aren't you boys from the Indian school?
And we'd ride home on the bus, walk in the door,
and surprise our mother. The second night we dreamed that,
moving and turning easily on our varnished pews
turning in our dreams to look out the bus windows
watching towns reversed from our trip north
time running backwards it seemed
a natural and right progression
(in the misplaced dreams of hopeful boys)
in the hopeful dreams of misplaced boys.

Grandmother at Indian School

Left on scrubbed wooden steps to think
about disobedience and forgetfulness
she feels warm sun on the back of her neck
as she kneels on the pale spot worn
by other little girls' tender knees,
a hundred black wool stockings
grinding skin and splintered wood,
beneath one knee a hard white navy bean.

Distant lightning flickers, nears, and
flashes down her shins, felt by other
uniformed girls marching to sewing class
waiting for their own inevitable return
to the stairs, to think and remember what happens
to girls who speak a pagan tongue.

Try to forget this pagan tongue.

Disobedient and forgetful she almost hears
beyond the schoolyard
beyond the train ride
beyond little girls crying in white iron beds

her mother far away
singing to herself as she cooks
speaking quietly with Grandma as they piece
the quilt for the new baby
and laughing with the aunties
while they wash clothes
  the little bean,
  does it hurt?

Bizaan, gego mawi ken, don't cry
she thinks, moving her knee so the little bean
feels only the soft part, and not the bone
    how long can I stay here?

And when Matron returns to ask if she's thought
she answers yes, I won't talk like a pagan again
and she stands and picks up the little bean
and carries it in her lonesome lying hand
until lights out,
when the baby bean
sleeps under her pillow.

The Canticle of the Night

Below the window a sheet glows
blue, as boy breathes a dream
melody, soft snores in and out,
his moonlit skin a lunar lavender;
he turns once, twice, sighs in sleep.

Across the room, unseen by the moon
the bed in the corner hidden in shadow
creaks, springs an assonant whine
as a restless sleeper kicks a gray wool blanket
from his soaring in the sky to earth.

Five other beds are gray shapes in the night
two lumpy mounds, two barely outlined bodies
the fifth a frightened dreamer who yelps,
flailing shadowed limbs into moonlight,
brown gray lavender blue
below round brilliance rising
higher and higher in the sky.

This night two boys wait, their breaths paired
below the cry below the snores
below the whine of bedsprings
below the moon's slow sail through the night.
Turned, their faces are mirrored
one in shadow one in moonlight
counting stars counting snores
counting hours days weeks

their breaths a soft descant
    one more night gone
    one more night
    one more gone
to the canticle of the night.

Saint Bernard

When I got to mission school
my worries about my mother
and how was she doing without me
had to wait when
the priest told me
I had a bigger worry than that.

When I died, he said,
they would never let me into heaven
when they heard my name.

With a name like mine, Barney,
not any kind of Bible name at all,
I couldn't float in
past the eyes of God.

He'd turn me away for certain
with a name like mine, Barney,
and send me back to mission school.

And so they named me after this big dog
who carried whiskey
in a little barrel around his neck
and saved people's lives
by bringing them a drink.

Well, I'd heard about that
and even saw it with my own eyes
in a bar in the West End.
Thanks, niijii, you saved my life,
a man told my uncle,
I was sure dying for a drink.

So I supposed it must be all right
and tried to feel the honor
of my namesake.

But it didn't stick
and I reverted to my pagan ways.
See, when I got home
and my mother said hello Barney
I was so happy
I forgot all about heaven.

Lugalette

One thing we never had at school was lugalette.
I always thought the word sounded so funny, LUGGLE-ette.
Some of the kids at school called it lug-o-lay,
some called it Indian bread or lug bread or just plain lug,
but they all knew what it was.

Back at home we had it every day, lugalette.
"What are you cooking, ma?" I would ask
just to hear her say "lugalette" and laugh.

Here's how you make lugalette:
Take enough flour to fill a good-sized bowl about half full
and mix in just a small handful of baking powder, some salt,
a bigger handful of sugar. Then draw a circle in it, to make
a little river, and mix in enough warm water or milk to make
a nice, soft dough. Knead the dough just a little, let it rest a
little bit, then put it in a greased pan and flatten it, careful,
with your hands. Bake it twenty–thirty minutes.

Some people cut the lugalette into squares before they bake it,
cut it into squares right in the pan, that makes it easier to break
into pieces after it's cooked. My mother used to slice it. You
can eat it hot or cold. If you've got some blueberries, you can
mix a handful into the dough, and that's good, too.
Mino pagwad.

Back home our mother made it every day.
We never had it at school, lugalette.
I always wished for it.

Bernadette

My first night at boarding school
the girl next to me in the dormitory
talked in Indian to me, asked me
just like the people at home
where was I from and who was my family
which comforted me. Then she said
don't wash your stockings yet,
we need the radiators.
Well, those girls took out the bread
they'd save from supper, and a jar of syrup
and said they were having a party for me,
the new girl. I'd never had a party before.

They taught me to make zip sandwiches.
Have you heard of them, zip sandwiches?
You take a piece of bread and pour a little syrup
and fold it and let it heat up and dry out
flat and hard on the radiator. Zip sandwiches.

Next time there was a new girl
sitting all sad and lonesome on her bed
I said after the matron was gone
"Aniin, ezhiyaa yaayaan?"
and told her to save her bread from supper
for a party that night. She smiled sideways.

Those zip sandwiches? Hard, stiff, sticky they were,
a little unsanitary I suppose, drying out
right where we would hang our underwear
after we'd washed it in the sink.
And flavor? Well, they didn't have much
but we loved them, and to this day, to me

when I eat any sweet, stiff, sticky food
it makes me think of those days,
and I taste kindness, and comfort,
the goodness and generosity of those girls.

Bruneaux

It was a good job.
Close to town. Regular pay.
Room and board. A good job.

Don't look at me, I wasn't the first one;
other Shinnobs had done it before me
and all things considered I didn't mind it
even if it was at a goddam Indian school.

The boys? They were all right, the boys,
and we all got along when they kept their noses clean.
And when they didn't, there wasn't anything new,
nothing I didn't see before, those hellish days
I was a boy at Indian school, myself.
Runaways fighters young
blanket-ass Indians sneaking around
like their ceremonies were a big secret from me
talking Indian under their breaths
like I couldn't understand what they were saying.
I took care of all that,
and when I caught some of them
having a little Indian dance out in the woods
I took care of that, too.

Every one that I beat
the ones who cried and the silent ones
the ones who broke
the ones who disappeared into themselves
they all acted like I didn't know myself
what a beating was. What did they think,
I was born knowing how?
I went to goddam Indian school, too.

Mary Remembering, on a July Afternoon

An afternoon like this reminds me of my grandma,
when she taught us how to bead
one summer. On a day like today, warm
she stretched carpet thread on a loom
ignoring the dishes, laundry, mending,
chores that could wait, those afternoons
the flowers grew beneath my grandma's hands.
Rough knuckles she had, and long-boned fingers
that lifted beads carefully from a jar lid
with her needle, counting
two blue two red eight white two red four green
four white four green two blue six white two blue.
A steamy afternoon it was at the table
where she sat flanked and squeezed
by me and Cynthia moving closer and closer
as we watched, pressing against her sides
yet she never said move away it was too hot,
only that the warm breath from our open mouths
limbered her fingers, softened the beeswax
with which she coated the thread,
and gave her a good grip on the sticky loom.

One day she gave us little wooden looms
she'd made, and our own needles, fast and silvery
to try out beading, and we felt honored
to do what Grandma did; honored
we watched and did what she did.
Threaded our looms
picked up beads with our needles
pressed up and wove
into no patterns at all, just beads,
but you know? She praised us,
praised us anyway, said that looks good.

It's been eighty years since I saw my grandma
but I remember when she taught us how to bead,
when flowers grew and bloomed beneath her hands
that summer just before my father died.

Mother in her sadness never sang
again, spending nights drinking days asleep
till the Indian agent noticed and sent me
to boarding school, where I was to forget
what Grandma taught me and learn other ways.

But, I remembered when she taught us how to bead,
that summer flowers grew beneath her hands
and when we brought our bracelets to town,
a long hot walk with Grandma to the store.
We sold our "just beads" bracelets for ten cents,
and Grandma got a dollar each for hers.
She said, you girls keep your money,
and bought blue yarn, brown sugar,
white cheesecloth, and three red suckers
for the long walk home, purchased
along with endless days, I would have thought,
of Mother singing as she sewed and cooked
of Father cutting pulp and hauling scrap
and Grandma, flanked and squeezed
between two small girls
who watched her work.

              I never did forget
that summer when she taught us how to bead,
when flowers grew and bloomed beneath her hands
and held it in my heart those lonely days
at school. Marching to class learning English
scrubbing the floors I held it in my heart,
that summer when she taught us how to bead,

those brown fingers, that soft gray dress, the steam
from summer heat, and learning-breathing mouths
limbering her fingers and the threads,
that summer Grandma taught us how to bead.

Abinoojiinh awi

Order

Bells at six.
Wash face and hands.
Brush teeth.
Hang the toothbrush on the hook with your initials next to it.
Gather clean stockings and underclothes from the radiator
school dress and apron from the hook on the wall
shoes from under the bed.
Air the bed.
Dress.
Comb, part, braid each other's hair.

Bells at six-thirty.
Line up.
March to the dining room.
Stand behind your chair.
At the signal, sit.
At the signal, pray.
At the signal, eat. Oatmeal. Coffee.
At the signal, rise. Line up. File out.
Place dirty dishes in the washtub next to the door.

Bells at seven.
Return to the dormitory.
Make bed.
Sweep.
Dust.

Bells at eight.
Line up.
March to the classroom.
Stand next to your desk.
At the signal, sit.
Lessons. Reading. Writing. Arithmetic. Penmanship.

Bells at eleven-thirty.
Line up.
March to the dining room.
Stand behind your chair.
At the signal, sit.
At the signal, pray.
At the signal, eat. Soup. Bread. Milk.
At the signal, line up. File out.
Place dirty dishes in the washtub next to the door.

Bells at twelve-thirty.
Line up. March to the dormitory.
Change into ticking-stripe work dress.
Hang school dress and apron on the hook next to the bed.

Bells at one.
Line up.
March to work.
Mondays, laundry.
Tuesdays, mending.
Wednesdays, ironing.
Thursdays, floors.
Fridays, sewing.

Bells at four-thirty.
Line up.
March to the dining room.
Stand behind your chair.
At the signal, sit.
At the signal, pray.
At the signal, eat. Beans. Potatoes. Bread. Blancmange.
At the signal, line up. File out.
Place dirty dishes in the washtub next to the door.

Bells at six.
Line up.

March to recreation.
Mondays, reading and letter writing.
Tuesdays, brisk walk around the school grounds.
Wednesdays, reading and letter writing.
Thursdays, brisk walk around the school grounds.
Fridays, dining room for group singing.

Bells at seven-thirty.
Line up.
March to the dormitory. Supervised free time.
> *Meni, you going home this summer?*
> *Louisa, lemme rat your hair for you,*
> *put it up like the white girls in town.*
> *Somebody help Zente polish her shoes.*

Bells at nine.
Change into nightgown.
Hang work dress on the hook next to the bed.
Place shoes under bed.
Wash underclothes and stockings in the lavatory sink,
hang them over the radiator to dry.
Wash.
Brush teeth.
Hang the toothbrush on the hook with your initials next to it.

Bells at nine-thirty.
Stand next to your bed.
At the signal, kneel.
At the signal, pray.
At the signal, into bed.
Lights out.
Silence.

Listen to the girl in the next bed cry.

Town, As I Recall It

Every other Saturday we got a ride to town from school
with our outing pay, sometimes two, three dollars
in our pockets, a lot of money in those days.

Mabel and me, we never looked at each other
but we were an item and I could see
she had curled the sides of her hair for the occasion.
I'd borrowed my brother's good pants; she could see that
though we never looked at each other.
In town we walked around together
looking in store windows, picking out things we liked.
We were an item, like I said. Once we almost touched
by accident, on my part. Mabel blushed
and looked at her shoes.

We went to school half-days and worked half-days.
Outing, they called it, or working out. Me, I worked
for a farmer who liked me; I was a hard worker,
and big. He called me "Buck" and let me drive his tractor,
a skittish thing wilder than a steer and a lot to handle,
rough riding on those iron tires but I enjoyed it.
When I got my money I wanted to buy something for Mabel,
who worked out as a mother's helper cleaning their house
wiping their kids' noses scrubbing laundry on a washboard
and their kitchen floors with a brush,
always with chapped hands.
They called it "working out" but she worked "in"
and she never made the kind of money I did.

In the dime store Mabel bought crochet thread
and I bought her a hair ribbon blue as the sky
because I knew she liked pretty things,
then I mailed a dollar to my mother.

We went to the show and sat in the dark
Mabel and me never touching, yet
across four inches of space and through
the papery starched whiteness of her blouse
I knew
    how did I know?
the tenderness of her carbolic-scented skin
cool tender Mabel whose resting fingers curved
in her lap around an invisible scrub brush
so bashful she looked straight at the screen
and obliquely past my eyes
to my hopeful aching self.

I remembered this after I left school
and during the war I remembered this
sitting in the dark with Mabel
inches from her gingery carbolic fragrance
watching the stagecoach make its way west

thinking one day I'd be like John Wayne
the Ringo Kid escaping jail for a better life
with the girl he would save from the bad guys
while Mabel in her starched cotton blouse
cool tender carbolic-perfumed Mabel
resting fingers curved in her lap
around an invisible scrub brush
as Kid and the Indians traded shots
half-smiled in the sweet darkness.

A pretty interesting place to be,
town, as I recall it.

Escape

There were certain things you could do to leave school.

Finish. Once you finished you could leave. Most didn't finish but some did. Some went on to another boarding school for high school or to learn a trade. Some stayed home, or because they didn't know what else to do.

Run away. Runaways and Indian schools always went together; you hear them mentioned together. A lot of kids tried it; a lot were caught. Runaways were easy to find because they all ran to the same place, home. Some the schools just let run without pursuit for a few days or a week, knowing where to find them. Sometimes when those kids arrived home they were met at the door by somebody from the school, the disciplinarian or even a teacher or the superintendent, who had been waiting for them. This saved everybody a lot of work. Some kids, though only a few, ran home and never went back to school, either because home was too far away to be worth the chase or because they ran so many times that the school got tired of the trouble.

Get sick. There was sickness at Indian school, that's for sure, and at every school. Measles, whooping cough, scarlet fever, impetigo all went through the schools and spread. Diphtheria. Influenza. Children sickened, recovered, sickened. The Spanish Flu closed whole schools down in 1919, and everybody was sent home. Trachoma wouldn't get you home, though you might be transferred to another trachoma school. You'd walk around with sore eyes all red and runny; you couldn't see straight. It could blind you eventually. T.B., tuberculosis, would get you out of school, but instead of going home you could get sent to a sanitarium

for your lungs to dry out and scar over.
And that's if you were lucky.
If you weren't you might go home
to give it to your family,
to cough and hemorrhage yourselves to death.

Die. You could die from getting sick, or you could die from
getting hurt. Accidents, sometimes; the teacher did not mean
for you to die when she pushed you down the stairs. There
were runaways who died from exposure or injuries. So
many ways to die. A boy kicked in the side by an angry
disciplinarian, another boy from pneumonia when he
wasn't allowed to sleep inside the dormitory. A little
girl with tuberculosis, sent home, her death thus not
counted in school reports to the government. A teenage
girl giving birth in the infirmary. A boy drowned swimming
in the lake. Children who died from broken hearts; they
were just too sad and homesick to eat, and couldn't live
without their mothers.

No promises were made that death would get you home;
instead, you might be buried at school,
your body cradled in the earth, and your spirit,
where is your spirit?
Amanj i dash.

Chi Ko-ko-koho and the Boarding School Prefect

From this owl's nest home, unsteady greasy oak
covered by cowhide long oblivious
to claws tough and curving as old tree roots
I breathe the night breeze, starry broken glass.

I am Chi Ko-ko-koho. My black-centered
unblinking owl eyes see past the dark
growl of this old bear den of a bar
through a stinging fog of unintended
blasphemy, tobacco's tarry prayers
stuck and dusty on a hammered tin ceiling
to grieving spirits mirrored by my own.

I am Chi Ko-ko-koho, young among owls
as young among lush crimson blooms of death
is the embryonic seedling in my chest
the rooting zygote corkscrew in my chest
these days all but unseen, a pink seaspray
sunset on a thick white coffee cup.
My grieving spirit hardly notices,
though, in this old bear den of a bar.

My owl head turns clear around when I see him.
I am Chi Ko-ko-koho; I blink away
smoke and fog, my head swivels back
and he's still there, the prefect. Still there
and he's real, not some ghost back to grab my throat
with those heavy no-hands of his
or crack my brother's homesick skinny bones
on cold concrete tattooed by miseries
of other Indian boys who crossed his path.

To the darkness of this bear den of a bar
he's brought his own sad spirit for a drink.

I am Chi Ko-ko-koho, but who he sees
is Kwiiwizens, a boy bent and kneeling
beneath the prefect's doubled leather strap
and Kwiiwizens I am. My belly feels
a tiny worm the color of the worm
writhe in laughter at my cowardice
as that now embodies ghost the old prefect
step-drags step-drags his dampened moccasins
to my end of the bar. Flowers weep rain
and embroidered beads in mourning for us all.

He asks me for a nickel for a beer.

With closed eyes Kwiiwizens waits for the strap
and I see them, the boy and the owl who are me.

Chi Ko-ko-koho dives from his grimy perch
to yank the apparition by the hair,
then flies him past the dark side of the moon
to drop him in the alley back behind
the dark growl of this old bear den of a bar.

Indizhinidaaz Kwiiwizens,
gaye indizhinikaaz Chi Ko-ko-koho.
Ni maajaa. Mi-iw. I leave him there.

I am Chi Ko-ko-koho. I leave him there
under stars of broken glass. I leave him there.

III

Anishinaabewi

The Refugees

To the dirging of "The Way We Were"
sung by some sweet girl nobody knows
six pallbearers
two in sweatshirts with faded logos
three in dress shirts, one with a tie
and one in a borrowed sportcoat
carry above their bowlegged lockstep mince
the green flocked vinyl coffin out the side door.
Inside she reposes, beloved mother, grandmother, aunt,
megis shell on a black string
wound over her bent brown fingers.

Six pallbearers worn as their boot heels
and ground to unassuming humility
by rounds of looking for work
and sometimes finding it gravely
wear their bodies as a single suit of clothes
fraying fast and worn at the knees.
These are faces of outside work, aging young skin
tanned by the sun and creased
ever more deeply season to season
filled and emptied filled and emptied
with grime and hard living
that search then escape what they'd found
spending night after night on a stool at Mr. J's
thinking, maybe after one more
I'll ask that blonde or her friend to dance;
no, guess I'll just go home, after all.

This is what happened to the other Indians,
not the airbrush-tanned noble savages you watch
on made-for-TV movies, running

in crisp, freshly ironed loincloths
through a pristine forest full of friendly animals
with an important message for the Chief
from his daughter the Princess,
who enthrall you so with their primitive ways
Oh wow these people are just so close to nature,
so SPEAR-itual (I wannabe, I wanna have)
that you can buy at a craft show stand
along with some gen-you-whine faux turquoise
jewelry so that you can be an Indian, too.

No, we're the other Indians,
the ones who did time in boarding school
where we learned to take a beating
never quite mastered the use of forced English
learned the work ethic and what it meant for us
but survived, more or less, in spite of it.

We moved to town, refugees we became
displaced persons scorned sometimes by our own.
Our daughters married white men
and learned to take a beating
never quite mastered Anglo housekeeping
lived the work ethic, and for them it meant
they would grow old early, our daughters
beloved and revered the bearers of life
and generations to come
how could we protect them, our daughters
whose bodies and spirits tired and whose
blue-eyed children went to public school
where they learned to take a beating
as well as give a beating in turn
never really mastered schoolwork,
leaving when they turned sixteen,

having learned what the work ethic meant for them
so they too could live hard and grow old early.

And today we're at another funeral,
and since it's the mortuary's rock-bottom budget
package deal we move outside the Sunset Chapel
once our hour is up. We're grateful
for this warm and sunny afternoon
and for room on the sidewalk
for cousins to meet and talk
("Ain't seen you since the last funeral")
till the chapel needs the sidewalk back
and we head for Mr. J's.

In repose our beloved is gone;
she has traveled her four-day spirit walk,
overcome her travails, and arrived west.
Her body waits in a green flocked vinyl coffin
on a shelf in the mortuary's garage
for the off-hours ride to the cemetery,
megis shell on a black string
wound over her bent brown fingers.

Gi gawaabimin, auntie.
We will see each other again sometime.

My Dad, Who Treated Life like a Sacrament

He drank the whole glass down all at once
    with respect
    eyes closed
    no stopping
and said to me
"There's nothing like milk, my girl"
and I could see
cows and green grass and sunshine
beautiful children with white teeth
all that might be
the good life it was
a sacrament right there for the taking.

The Beanbag

When snow began to thaw, at first we saw
only a trace of flowered calico,
then every day more cotton flowers bloomed,
deep blue blossoms wet with melting snow.
Familiar, it looked. I remembered
forget-me-nots on her favorite house dress
that, when worn out, she crocheted with a hook
into a rug, mostly; the smallest scrap
she sewed into a child's toy, a beanbag.

I remember that dress.
As a child, when she held me close,
my face against her soft, flowered middle
smelling starch and warm geranium
in her soft and cool fleshy embrace
I felt small, an infant, or not yet
born, in a cocoon of blue-flowered cloth.

Early in the spring after she died
one day I recognized that flowered dress:
forget-me-nots on cotton, wet buds of blue flowers
on a beanbag we were kicking around the yard.

Split, it spilled the past

    Her kitchen floor,
    bumpy patterned linoleum, shiny and bare
    reflecting wavy geraniums in coffee cans,
    nurtured from seeds of their own great-grandmothers
    checked oilcloth
    leaned to white pearl scallops at the edge
    by her daughters' slender, bending waists
    and ground to silver dollars, several pairs,

by her ravenous sons' elbows
kitchen woodstove a hot dull black
bread baking in the oven;
above, noodles boiling tomatoes roiling
singing huffs of steam above our heads

I remember when the beanbag spilled the past;
when it split and spilled the past I remembered,
and picked it up, to see it one more time

and what was that? I looked close, and closer.
Through its frayed weave of returning to the earth
the bag held life beyond the tiny past.
Split and spilt, its damp side finely pierced
by an infant seedling yet blind, but greedy
for the light, born in a cocoon of flowered
blue calico, a pattern wet with melting snow
forget-me-nots an early sign of spring
entwined with a trace of tender green.

I remember her flowered dress,
that dress.

Mewinzhaa, Bijiinaago: Linda and Uncle Ray

(walks in the front door, cracked dark varnish beads
around an oval glass. hangs her coat on the stairpost.
her mother says here, bring this to your Uncle Ray.
carries a plate of buttered soda crackers to the table,
watches him pour soup from the tin saucepan into the
pink-flowered bowl for her, the chipped green one for
himself. two spoons. he gives her the shiny one.)

"When I went to school we didn't walk home for dinnertime."
"Did you live too far away?"

(train ride. lye soap. penmanship. blots and a ruler to
bruised knuckles. no tears. loading hay with a pitchfork.
Zane Grey in the reading room. a box of cookies from a
missionary on Christmas Day. a visit from ma and the
old man. unbearably contained joy in a muted practiced
handshake. speaking English, Zhaaganaashiimowin.
hello sir, hello mother, we have been very well here.)

"Stayed there for suppertime, too."
　　(she is too small to know this)
"It was a different kind of school."
　　(curiosity) (?) (she lifts his rain-dampened plaid wool
　　jacket from the back of the kitchen chair and drapes
　　it over the radiator to dry.)
"Want some more soup?"
　　(love for a small girl with short braids)

The Invisible Child

Teacher, I'm quiet here at my desk
looking down you think
at an empty lined worksheet,
my chapped fingers with bitten nails
holding a pencil that's lost its eraser
so I can't make mistakes, and I'm no trouble to you
at all, hiding behind a white girl in a pretty dress.

You don't see my spirit leave this desk
to fly like a bat out of hell through the halls
rehearsing cannonballs, loop-the-loops, skyrockets
for the day you might see me, when I become real
the day I find the updraft and really do fly.

I'm undersized and quiet, mousy you think
and it irritates you to see me puffing my mouse cheeks
while I read at my desk. You don't know it's my teeth
my teeth a painsong accompanying what I do
     when they hurt too much I get one pulled
     and the nails in my shoes rise into my heels
     and my wash-worn socks fall into my shoes
     all winter my cold makes me talk so kids laugh
     and my family's so big you make jokes about us
     right at me and I don't get it, teacher.
Don't know what sex is or birth control but I know it's a joke.
Sometimes I laugh too so you can't see
my eight-year-old feelings hurt, but you can't see.

Teacher, who's more ignorant, you or me?

I'm quiet and undersized and no trouble at all,
behind that girl in the pretty dress. Watching your world

I listen to you and think about you too
as my spirit flies like a bat through the halls
unseen, teacher, unseen until the day I become real
the day I find the updraft and really do fly.

Miss Shawn

I am afraid of that deceptive face
    handsome dark-eyed intelligent
    in structure a sheep's face or a camel's
    with an animal's acceptance and dignity
    that masks a cruel soul I have seen before
but even more of that melodic voice
a deep and long-vowelled cello song oozing
through a beige throat draped by long folds of skin
two knobs at its fearsome base, and to its
menacing and oddly tuneful hypnotic beat
"Linda LeGarde" I rise as learned the hard way
to stand at the right side of the desk
eyes front straight ahead face to face with Miss Shawn
chilled by the meter of that voice
my left hand touching home, my desk
fixed and stable, warm wood with floral iron grillwork
a trellis passage to the tranquility and safety
of sitting behind the boy who blocks her view of me
but I have risen now and stand exposed
eyes front straight ahead face to face with Miss Shawn.

"Your family is Indian. What tribe are you people from?"

And while above thirty-three other iron-trellised desks
pale faces turn to watch the glare of my misery
curious and glad it's not them, at the thirty-fourth desk
the other Indian child in class looks away,
sympathic and sorry it's my turn. He knows;
he's had more than his share. I stand
exposed and in need of cover
    try not to look afraid

eyes front straight ahead face to face with Miss Shawn
 and can't look down, that's not allowed
as she takes two steps and I can't help it
my eyes drop and I can see it all so clearly.

Brown leather teacher shoes with chunky heels. Two extra
pairs on the shelf by her desk. Brown teacher dress, chunky
pin over the left breast. More teacher dresses gray beige
maroon in her closet at home. Teacher car in the parking
lot, tan Chevy with tan upholstery. It has a spare key and
a spare tire. She's never had a flat. Never run out of gas.
Her house is large and everybody sleeps in beds. Her garden
is for decoration with no pit for burning trash. When she gets
bored she talks about these things and sometimes her college
days, spent on the moon for all I understand what she's
talking about.

My uncle, who went to Indian school awhile and got left
behind. My uncle, kinder more decent certainly smarter and
more interesting than Miss Shawn. My brothers and sisters
who would have to have Miss Shawn for sixth grade after me.
My dad teaching us kids the most important word in the
Chippewa language, migwech. Indians. Chippewas. Visiting
joking laughing. My aunt setting her mother's hair.

 "Nindaanis, are them pincurls good and tight?"
 "So tight, Ma, you won't be able to shut your eyes."

My cousin, who got slapped by his teacher for not speaking.
Timmy, the other Indian child in class, getting slapped
by Miss Shawn for smiling during singing time. Miss Shawn.

I don't want to tell her.

Exposed, I look for shelter with a lie.
"Navajo."

"Oh. NAH vuh ho." Amazingly, she says that I may sit down. And I have survived unharmed, to take my place again behind the boy who blocks her view of what I see.

It's not such a bad day at school, after all.

Ann's Market SALADA TEA

a love poem from Duluth's West End

_____

Gilt words on a corner-store window
painted by a salesman they had likely outlived
Ann's Market SALADA TEA
reflected street light and sun,
bright against the steamy green of houseplants
that obscured the inside.

We just called it "Ann's."

From the sidewalk the store looked dark;
inside, eyes adjusting
to the dim lighting, naked bulbs
on cords hung from a time-darkened tin ceiling
blinked twice, pupils widened,
then the child (sent by his mother for bread)
or the stevedore (out of milk and snoose)
or the lonely widow (needing some company)
could see it all right to the back,
to the flowered calico curtain
obscured her private life
from the rest of the West End.
Alive, the curtain looked
alive as the plants in the window
when the small freezer
yellow-gray, scratched and etched glass top
surged on with groans and wheezes
as it maintained the solidity
of nickel Popsicles, and thirty-cent pints of ice cream
vanilla, chocolate, and Neapolitan,

called Napoleon by old West Enders.
The freshest thing in the store
was the rack of Taystee Bread
refilled by the bread man once a week
who took the unclaimed orphan loaves
to the day-old store.
Warm, dark
wood floor creaking
freezer snuffling,
by day Ann's was mellow.

But after school the place was jumpin'
when Lincoln Junior let out and the kids
(young greasers we admired Connie and Skeeter,
Elvis, Conway, and Jerry Lee)
rocked and rolled through the door,
flocks of freed blackbirds and sparrows
lighting at Ann's glass penny candy case,
the biggest in the West End.
Ann sat behind the counter, on a rickety stool,
wearing a cotton housedress, one day plaid,
the next a gray floral that matched the curtain,
waving her scepter, a broom handle
and telling us to behave or get out!
Her favorite kids waited on themselves
sliding the glass doors back and forth
taking orders and handing out licorice and Chum Gum
while Ann collected the money, you paid on your honor
which worked fine if you weren't fussy
as the candy wasn't wrapped
and passed through unwashed hands.
On a winter day I got in the store last,
in the last row of the flock,
candy-craving crows and sparrows
shrieking for Jolly Ranchers and taffy

I waited at the window of summer green,
my backside against the radiator
the cactus brushing the back of my coat,
for my penny piece of pickle gum
that looked like the cactus.
Sticky and fuzzy on the tongue,
it tasted of sweat and pennies and wool mittens.

In high school we grew worldly,
crows and sparrows muted to doves and ravens
rolling eyes at the after-school invasion into Ann's.
Callow, self-conscious sophisticates we agonized
over Diane liking Greg who liked Karen who liked Bob
and the new boy at the Wesley Church parsonage
just down the hill from Ann's.
Girls whispered behind their hands
about his smile, his button-down collars,
his English-looking shoes
from Dayton's in Minneapolis, we'd heard,
that shy minister's son innocent of West End ways.
A lovely autumn evening in the West End it was
when he and Ann met; a quarter passed
from his palm to hers, the exchange
the purchase of a loaf of Taystee Bread.
Her mouth opened when he asked for a bag.
"What do you think that little thing on the end is for?"
she asked, which began his education
as a West End boy. I heard about it.
I had noticed him, of course,
and one day he noticed me.
And on a cindery West End summer night
walking like other boys and girls did
from Ann's to the wilds of Lincoln Park,
down to Penney's to look in the windows,
then to the library on Second Street

and back to Ann's, we fell in love,
like other boys and girls did in the West End.
We shared a near-beer, tentative and shuffling,
quiet and close on the gritty sidewalk
that reflected the moon to a million bitty stars,
then looked up at the real stars against the sky
so dark and soft, watching them shine for us
as big and bright as they did
for the people in far and foreign East End,
countless stars free as the Taystee bread from Ann's
was for people who really needed it, miraculous stars
unknown light years away reflecting back shining gold
in the window of
Ann's Market SALADA TEA

The Class of 1968

Ten little, nine little, eight little Indians,
seven little, six little, five little Indians,
four little, three little, two little Indians,
one little Indian . . .

and that left me the last one
of the bunch, kindergartners of 1955
our teachers our varied shades of skin our histories
those random chances silent banshees chasing children
the only one left, and the one perceived as leaving

Leaving Vicky, pregnant in the eighth grade,
    who never came back
Vernon and George, nomads
     between reservation and town
     'til they were forgotten
Wanda, always sick and agonizingly shy,
    who disappeared
Birdeen, who went to work after her father died
Percy and John, expelled for fighting
and Susan for skipping school
     to care for the younger kids at home
Jim, who studied incorrigibility at juvenile hall
Pete, who advanced that study at Red Wing
Eliza, who never learned to read
     and waited for her sixteenth birthday
Bonita, who almost made it but "had to" get married,
     as we said in 1968

and that left me the last one
the forgotten the untouched the protected
the bookish the lucky the lonely
the last one.

Mary Susan

Our little sister was named after an aunt who died before we were born. Aunt Mary Susan was a young girl, a student at a South Dakota mission school near the Wounded Knee Massacre in 1890. The nuns at the school, hearing that something bad was going on, took the children outside to a ditch where they spent the night. They survived.

Mary Susan returned to Minnesota, where she married, had five children, and was widowed. Left with a family to support, she found a job as a cook at the Vermilion Lake Indian School, then spent all of her working years with boarding school children. My dad remembers her as a generous woman, only as tall as a child, who spoke softly and kindly. He honored her memory by naming our little sister after her.

Our little sister was the only blonde in our family. As children we were fascinated by her coloring, her hair that lightened to an ice frost in the summer, her cheeks that bloomed with a red fire in the winter. Winters she became the sun; summers, the moon. We masked our anger and humiliation at neighbors' stupid jokes about the stork, the wrong baby, the mailman, by pretending we didn't understand. She was our sister, we could see that. We were photo negatives, reversals of the same black and white image, a bone structure and history interchangeable under skin, eyes, and hair.

In the early 1970s an Indian Club was started at our high school. What an event that was, an organization that would acknowledge and support Indian ways in an institution that had stood for the annihilation of our people through education/assimilation. Our little sister went to Indian Club until picture day, when the other students asked her to step off the riser and out of the camera's

eye because with her coloring she wouldn't match the group on
the yearbook page.

After that she always felt like she stood out in pictures.

Winters she became the sun, summers the moon.
In all seasons our sister and our auntie's namesake.

For Asin

Eyes down sitting alone he is
below the salt outside the pale beyond the tracks
he is a twelfth grade Indian boy eating his lunch
unseen on the steps outside the school.
His parents are proud his cousins envious
of the accomplishments of this invisible boy
this solitary warrior who is a silent apparition
not seen not heard not known
by other students flirting and horsing around
on the steps after lunch unaware of the warrior,
those laughing girls in important peasant chic
and teasing boys in jeans and chambray shirts,
the proletarian kitsch of 1973.
Eyes down he eats two vapor sandwiches
and folds the brown paper bag into his pocket
then walks into school unnoticed,
a ghost floating past the guidance counselor's office.

This morning the ghost took human form
for the counselor, who with shortsighted eyes saw
an Indian boy head down too shy unappealing
frayed shirt bad teeth a C student.

> *I was wondering about college, said the warrior.*
> *It isn't for everyone, said the counselor.*

Below the salt outside the pale beyond the tracks
unseen in silence the invisible warrior walks point.
He is a woodland warrior in a foreign jungle,
camouflaged in wash pants and frayed shirt,
a C student with bad teeth and downcast eyes
the pride of his parents the envy of his cousins
the hope of his brothers and sisters, walking point

leaving tracks the impossible shimmer of our dreams,
tracks that trade the shade of the sky the hue of tomorrow
through the foreign jungle across cracked concrete
up the stairs through the Age of Aquarius crowd
to college.

Asin, you walked before us.
Asin, in your memory and honor
we now rise to our feet and walk
step after step in your tracks
that we broaden to a path
the shade of the sky
the hue of tomorrow
the shimmer of your dreams.

Asin, in your memory and honor
visible now we walk.

Lost and Astigmatic Twenty-Nine-Year-Old Self

As the sign on the door says
printed in bright green crayon on cardboard

    YOU ARE HERE
    SOBRIETY POWWOW
    EVERYBODY WELCOME

and here you are indeed
in 1979, in Onigamiising
in a Methodist church social hall
with your father, who
hearing the drum and singing, brightens
and your three little girls
in matching denim bib overalls and ironed, ruffled blouses,
here you are

    YOU ARE HERE

squinting at an unclear world from behind thick lenses
(the world will focus in time, but how can you know this,
twenty-nine-year-old lost and astigmatic self?)
holding your smallest child's hand and your father's arm

at a sobriety celebration gathering
under institutional fluorescent light fixtures
that on this overcast afternoon
mimic the paleness of the sun glowing through clouds.

As there is beauty
in the pallid light of sun shining through clouds
so there is beauty
in the touching mimicry of the fluorescent lights

in the feast of Indian hot dogs, wild rice, jello, cake,
powdered orange drink and coffee coffee coffee
in the dancers, some in street clothes
some in Indian clothes (as we called them in 1979)
all there in honor of the sobriety warriors
and the warriors, themselves, proud
modest battle-scarred ogichidaa spirits
a little embarrassed by the attention
and the old man who called to my dad
"Jerry LeGarde!"
then spoke to him in Indian
(my dad answered and they conversed,
to my surprise; I didn't know he could do that
and perhaps this is as long and familiar a story
to you as it is to me; if not I will explain sometime)
and the lineup for the food, with the Elders eating first
and Grand Entry, the prayers, the Veterans song
and the m.c. who made everybody laugh
after a really good song,
so good that everybody in the room got up to dance.

"That was an old traditional song of our people
called 'When I Get My Payment'!"
he announced into the mic,
Indianishly (as we said in 1979)
tempering (as we still do)
extremes of happiness sadness
light darkness the ugly and the beautiful
and the inevitably increasing clarity that each day brings
with a joke.

Lost and astigmatic twenty-nine-year-old self,
the directions you sought were printed in bright green crayon
on cardboard taped to the doors of a church social hall

YOU ARE HERE
SOBRIETY POWWOW
EVERYBODY WELCOME

There you were
and here you are.

IV

Gichi-Anishinaabewi

Loss and a Question

For times when there appeared to be no good solution
or answer my father lightened things up with
a line from Robert Frost's "Love and a Question":
"Stranger, I wish I knew," he would say.

————————

". . . but before we begin
we need to acknowledge
that the land we stand upon
was traditionally occupied
by the [name your tribes]
from time immemorial but
who don't occupy it anymore
because it is now ours. Their
culture is amazing, by the way."

Settler, what might be this need
on your part
to acknowledge
if that is even the right word
that we are standing on land,
settler, you and I,
that you state is now yours?

Thank you
You're welcome
Don't rub it in
(weak smile)
(Ojibwe style head nod)
Settler, welcome to the homeland
Gaawiin; none of these seem right.

Shall we quote the saddest of lines
sung by Buffy Sainte-Marie:
"Hands on our hearts we salute you your victory"

or shall we kneel?

How many of these
land acknowledgment statements
that are in truth
land acquisition statements
have I listened to,
the coldness of reality
delivered earnestly righteously
or crowing perhaps
with a triumphantly virtuous
preening of feathers
or that one time
by a young Native woman
not in a position to refuse
the peculiar honor
who though somewhat uneasy
maintained dignity
and self-respect for us all?

Is there a proper response
to a land acknowledgment
land acquisition statement
and all that has followed that loss
displacement deprivation starvation
removals broken families
disrupted dreams lives destroyed
absent children dying far from home
alcoholism trachoma tuberculosis
rolling through decades, centuries,
in the wake of your acquisition of land,

your acknowledgment statement
feeble futile and for what reason and need?

Settler, I wish I knew.
My spirit spirals in the wake of ancestors
then pauses; I look at the sky
questioning while day passes
dusk falls stars look down
amanj, amanji i dash
and I don't know, and I wonder
what would Elders
whose advice I would seek
if they were not absent
bodies gone to the next world
or minds preceding the physical journey,
what would they counsel?

"They are our guests,"
an old man once said to me,
"guests on this land
and we treat them the way you do
when somebody comes to the house,
invite them inside, offer them a place to sit,
share what you have, that's our way.
Wherever anybody goes, we are either guests
in their house, or they are a guest in ours
and that's how the Ojibwe do it.
The Creator made us to be that way."

Gii-gikenjige, geget.
Birthed long before the question
the response is our existence,
the continuity of our ways
by breath and heartbeat
learning and teaching

words and deeds
we are the lifeblood
linking ancestors and descendants.

Settler, biindigen; namadabin; wiisinin.
Aniin miinik? I wish I knew.

Casualty Days

Back in the world as summer passed
through bright and gritty dog days, tethered girls
captured faceless voices and placed calls
pairing braided coiled snakes red white
gray white across the continent,
Sharon to Missoula, Pam to New York
their sad and tender fingers glittering
in the absence of their men who slept, it seemed
to the girls on second shift it almost seemed
they slept in jungles off the China Sea.

I passed them on the sidewalk outside Bell,
some college kids home on their summer break
girls in hippie dresses and peasant chic
boys in blue chambray work shirts and jeans
feigning righteousness sitting crossed-legged
(Indian-style, they thought) on the sidewalk
singing and chanting *"Ho Ho Ho Chi Minh!*
NLF is gonna win!" A white girl
costumed ersatz Indian princess
who wore a beaded headband from Japan
looked right through me, a Native working girl
in nylons, carrying a vinyl purse.

Upstairs we plaited spiderwebs of calls.
"Solidarity forever; our union makes us free"
floated up on humid summer air
to our window and over the switchboard,
weighting the hands and hearts of anchored girls,
unseen sisters of the working class.

And sleepless girls we sang through the night
songs I remember as I remember our fright

Operator.
Your number, please?
Please deposit five cents more.
Operator.
Your number, please?
I'm sorry, ma'am, your time is up.

Remember, Bev, how very young we were?
I remember, and remember that he'd kissed your pretty face.
I remember your blue eyes and waiting face.

And Bev, remember those "casual wear days"
when operators who'd met their quotas
were rewarded with potluck lunches
and freed from polyester working clothes
for a day of being someone not ourselves?
In jeans we almost looked like college girls.

That summer day so fragile you maintained,
chilled and sweatered, gratefully talking
recipes with the older operators,
kind ladies their spreading flesh fading and
Tussy-scented inside their casual wear,
picnic "wash" dresses soft with wear and age.
Polite and frightened we spooned and swallowed
uneasy noodle salads, their intended comforts
our reward for being such good and grownup girls.

Remembering themselves in other wars
they knew, they knew how young we really were.

Summer passed; days shortened and grew cold.
Migratory birds and college kids
soared and disappeared into the sky.

Here in the world we hurried to work
in thin-soled flats light on the frosty sidewalk
to punch in and anchor to the switchboard,
bound and faceless girls weaving America
red white gray white across the continent
Duluth to Detroit, to the fire department,
to the Busy Bee Market. Business. Births. Deaths.

Bev, that January casual wear day
you were pale and thin, fragile in winter white.
Beneath the bowl held out on the palm of your left hand
your diamond ring, loose, spun and caught the light.
That day, white marble balanced on an egg
as flatly jazzed bridal lasagna sweat
unsteady beads through wedding gift Pyrex embellished
with gold roosters flaunting avocado plumes
while shivering girls tiptoed past their bloom.

Kathy's cave rat tunneling deep in the jungle
and Sharon's sniper in that twelve-foot boat,
in sleep, those absent boys, what did they dream
while their feet softened yellowed, damp
in heavy laced boots, near the China Sea?
And your own soldier, Bev, lost there in the fog
within the greenest of jungles woke dreaming of you.

Remember, Bev, how very young we were?
I remember, and remember that he'd kissed your pretty face.

Ikwe Ishpiming

From black of light years asi anong
writhed and spiraled into his path,
shedding sparks that dazzled his eyes.
He raised one arm to shade his face
and began to dance, unaware that he danced
while above I flew, gold in the sky.
With my hair the wind I tethered his wrists
to a shining cloud as I silently swayed
and breathed in the wind, ambe, ambe.
My hands the earth that gave him life
bathed his feet in shredding silk
that tore in my touch as I whispered
ambe omaa, bimosen, bimosen.
Then my lips rained silver sand that poured
into the river that rolled from its sleep
and I spoke through the water, wewiib, wewiib
till he followed, filling my tracks with his own.

Parturition, a Poem for Brenda and Terrie

Having won the game of patience seven times
    and lost four
I re-rubberband the deck
    my legs writhe restlessly, straighten
and rise wobbily to stand on dusty gray linoleum tiles
    soles balance my weight, my soul my wait
which pleases the labor room nurse (who holds all power)

    "Look how limber she is! Jumped right off that bed!
    Good idea, walk … walk … that'll get that baby out!
    Ring if you need me!"

from a great distance it seems she bubbles
and waves, and waves

thus grounded perhaps in control of my destiny,
the sullen indignities of these hours cumbrous
on my unseen feet yellow with cold I imagine
that walk a crescent fertile and horseshoe-shaped
around the bed and back, around and back;
above, my yet unbirthed motherspirit
listens to seasons from the swimmer within.

After countless paced crescents she startles me,
an old woman with lined elm bark face and calm eyes
watching me through a small window in the wall

    "Grandmother?" I wonder, heartened
    by this visit I have wished for in my dreams
    since the day she died two months
    into my own conception

then realize the window is a mirror,
and I an ageless crone at twenty-two.

In that dimension past where numbers end
but not this walk and wait, yoked to this time
and clutching to each hip a fabric bouquet
blue fleur-de-lis on a tattered hospital gown
barefoot left crescent turn right crescent turn
as the waves crest break recede, crest break recede
and halt
silence.

    Where are the seasounds?

I have worn a shining silver omega
that frames the bed, gray linoleum buffed
and polished by my blessedly pain-free feet
that now step cautiously past my cronehood
and syncopate dustily toward my husband,
who sleeps in a harvest gold vinyl chair with chrome legs

    "Can you hear that?" I inhale to form the words
    "I can't hear the seasounds anymore."

but in that breath the swimmer turns, the silence breaks
with a pop as water rushes, flooding my cold yellow feet
with warm waves that carry dust bunnies
from beneath the bed to the corners of the room
out the door and down the corridor
to the nurses' station.
I complete my inhalation. Should I ring?

    "Did you hear something?" my husband asks
    through the pitch of the rippling sea
    "Did you hear something?" he asks the girl I used to be.

Lisa, Let Us Remember Richard

Do you remember Richard's hands, Lisa?
Michelangelo caught and stilled hands like Richard's,
his Adam's frescoed reach bound by two dimensions
that on Richard were four—height depth breadth time
    lives before us lives yet to come
    assailed existence onerous survival
    not regarded as art or beauty, although
    it is a beauty rougher than fresco
    and warm as wood, if wood were flesh
    elegantly crafted walnut with oil finish
delicately poised for work or rest, unaware
that surgeons, musicians, artists
would weep in envy at the sight

but there was more to this.
Richard's demeanor bespoke his hands
tentative, unobstrusive, and with a tremor so slight
that gave Richard's hands an animation, life
that joined and sang with the spirits who dwell
in pencils, spoons, split wood, rawhide.

Lisa, let us remember
the late summer afternoon
he sat on the back stairs, making a drum.
We watched his hands hollow a stump
and stretch, coaxingly, wet rawhide
while my little girls and Richard's nieces
played on the swing set in the yard.
"Uncle Richard washed our hair last night,"
said Peaches. "For bugs; they're all gone now,"
said Kitty. Richard looked up and smiled as
those hands that had gently washed and combed

lice from little girls' hair shaped and smoothed
wet rawhide to a ragged circle then laced
top and bottom back and forth, back and forth.

Do you see this photograph? Do you remember
I walked among the children with a roasting pan
of watermelon wedges that late summer day?
Out of the frame you stood by in a yellow apron,
holding a glass of wine and looking upward.
Was it cloud pictures you saw forming and re-forming
of the last season's rice harvest,
Richard newly sober and newly strong;
were you listening for the sky song of jigging day?
Braced against the open car door
he sang with the sky, dancing on dried hulls.

We sat on the back stairs watching the children play
while Richard carved the drumstick, the air cool
in the afternoon shade; I recall damp wood
and peeling paint soft and curving under our backsides,
the piece of sheepskin the color of the clouds
that his beautiful hands wrapped onto the drumstick.

The dog, smitten by the smell of Richard and rawhide,
nosed and kissed his hands, and slept at his feet.

Lisa, let us remember winter,
that afternoon we had a flat.
As Richard changed the tire under a sun the color of clouds
we stood behind him to cut off the icy wet wind.
"Makes me wish I had some gloves;
it's hard on the hands," he half-laughed in his quiet voice
as his fingers stiffened to hardwood
from the touch of that cold cold iron jack.

Later on we walked along the tracks checking snares
 and I remember it like a photograph
 Richard in his red plaid lumberjacket
 arms crossed, hands in his armpits
 you in your long dressy coat
 me in my mother's quilted jacket
and found a rabbit caught but still alive
struggling it paused then kicked, paused then kicked
"I hate when this happens," Richard said
in his quiet voice; bending and turning away
to spare the sight of what was necessary,
mercifully and quickly tightening the wire
with his kind and sorrowing hands.

At Richard's place, Donna made the soup
and frybread so light it danced on the plate
(we didn't know a white girl could do that).
"What do you use, baking powder or soda?"
we aspiring Frybread Queens asked.
"I use both," said rosy Donna,
all bashful as an Indian.
"I taught her how," said Richard
as Donna charmed golden puffs from the stove.

Then with warmed hands the color of the frybread
and rough and graceful as the old wood table we sat at
he served us all, his elderly father first.
Feasting, we listened to Richard's dad, veteran and elder
with Richard's distant, husky voice
tell us about when he was in the army,
stationed in the South years ago, after the war,
and all the mixed-blood people down there.
"Good to us, the Makadewisug; always
nice to Indians, and fed us, too.

A lot of them part-Indian, themselves, you know;
treated us nice and shared their food with us."

In the spring Richard showed us how to cut porcupine quills
under a plastic bread wrapper, with toenail clippers
so the little points wouldn't fly up
and put out our eyes.
He made us quill necklaces light as air
that rested on our collarbones, singing his songs.

He wrote me once after I moved away
on a card he'd bought especially,
with a sketch of an Indian woman on it.
He hoped all was good and that I liked the picture

and then he moved, too,
to Minneapolis, near the Ave,
and was lost

I ran into his sister after that
and she said I wouldn't know if I saw him
that he was killing himself drinking

Lisi-ens, sometimes I do it, too,
step out of the frame and look skyward
where for all we know it is possible
that we might see Richard
in the clouds.

To the Woman Who Just Bought That Set of Native American Spirituality Dream Interpretation Cards

Sister, listen carefully to this.
You'll probably walk right past me
when you're looking
for a real gen-you-whine
mythical traditional Indian princess
to feed
delectably
and flagellate
delectably
your outrage and un-guilt
about the way other people
not as woke and sensitive as you
did to women
by the way, women like me
who you probably walk right past
when you're looking.

I know what you're looking for
and I know I'm not it.
You're looking for that other Indian woman
you want
a for-real gen-you-whine
mythical traditional princess
and you'll know her when you see her
glibly glinting silver and turquoise
carrying around her own little
magic shop of real gen-you-whine
jangling charms and rattling beads
beaming about her moon
as she sells you a ticket to her sweat lodge.

She's a spiritual concession stand
and it's your own business go ahead and buy
or rent it if you want to go ahead
and acquire what you will,
you've done it before.
I know what you're looking for
and I'm not it. Happily invisible
I won't be dressing up or dancing for you
or selling you a ceremony
that women around here have never heard of
I won't tell your fortune
or interpret your dreams
so put away your money.

Sister, you weren't listening to this
I know, and I know too that
you are looking past me
and women like me,
thank goodness is all we can say
for that authentic, guaranteed
satisfaction or your money back
gen-you-whine
mythical traditional Indian princess.

What you are really looking for
you'll never find and anyway
it's not for sale.

Nindaaniss Waawaashkeshiikwesens on a Winter Night

In the moonlight quiet of a winter night
as I pass by her bedroom door
nindaaniss Waawaashkeshiikwesens
my daughter the deer girl
springs from her bed.
From the distant dark forest of her sleep
she totters to my arms,
her wide dark eyes asking, "What? Wegonen?"
and I carefully lead her back to her bed.
"My girl, shh, ssh, nibaan, nibaan,
go to sleep, go back to sleep."
Folding her slender deer legs
she nestles under the pile of blankets
I tuck around her
and her wide dark eyes close
as she returns to the distant dark forest sleep
Of the waawaashkeshiiwag.

Anishinaabikwe–Everywoman

He Inini

> Native man who seeks the Great Mystery
> looks longingly out the window
>> past the birds and trees
>> into his own mind
> long hair hiding his back.

I Ikwe

> Native woman so close to Mother Earth
> protect him from this cruel and mundane life
>> with hard work courage and love
>> my strengths
> while my feet never leave the ground.

My quest never began
and his will never end.

Looking for a Woman with the Blues

he was looking for a woman with the blues,
the blue blue blues of a woman wronged
so blue in the glass we sang our sad songs
as he picked up his guitar and strummed along

he drove in behind a bucking bronc, defeat
in rusting mirrored triumph strutting
bravado offerings of self-loathing, no free lunch
for sad women in a dark and noisy bar, while she

grieving past competition won hands down,
a doe downed gutted consumed by fire
ashes blown across blackened, ice-covered ruins
singed rose lace curtains ruffled in the snow

then banshee clouds tattooed by purple thumbs
broke to women swimming up in smoke
that tasted of the hot blue fires of hell
but the winner was the saddest of us all
he'd found himself a woman with the blues

Nanaboozhoo

women bring him things
bits of paper with little notes
coffee mugs hip clever sneakily domestic
dead mice from the field
we can't help our nature
we'd catch him if we could
but we can't
nevertheless
we leave small corpses
hopeful offerings
at the doorstep

Magdalene in the Shade of Veronica's Love

She kneels, covering his feet with her long hair,
this young and ruined woman weeping her regrets.

He takes her hand and she rises, forgiven;
the repentant beauty of her face fills his eyes.

Within the void that is the watching crowd
my hands ache, curving like claws
reach but touch nothing
but the reluctant sorrowing mystery.

So long ago, before time mortified my soul,
young I begged strangers for an imprint
that their hands their lips might mark my existence
that is now manifest in the inconsequentiality
of my cronehood, the lines of my face
the whiteness of my hair
my mottled hands misshapen fingers.

Now in imposed silence
hard earned hard learned
the question is mute, or moot.
Where is the absolution
for the inconsequential spirit?
And is the question of any consequence?

Shame and salvation.
I would gather her pain
to my betrayed and tender waste.
I would weep if I could
but can only sway
above her disarming, guileless grief.

E. W. Bohannon, My Grandmother, and Me

E. W. Bohannon rests upright under glass,
blind blue gaze dignified and detached, calmly
afloat on a pale sea, enigmatic doldrums
of cured oil beiges contoured
on a flat stretched canvas.

More often than I should I pause here,
my rushed steps down this tiled, wax-dusted hall
slowed, drawn to the painterly portrait
of this long-dead educator

and my own superimposed reflection,
shadowed palimpsest that traces a third face
silent planes of my own grandmother's
whose years (and her children's)
at boarding schools .
Red Lake Mission
Tomah
Hayward
Vermilion Lake
Red Lake Government
Pipestone
coincided with E.W.'s tenure and now
collide in the layering of countenances

pondering his academic gown hood demeanor
and his civilized world of books and order
preserved in oils now dry
and fragile as his flesh and bones
long moldered to powder underground
in darkness to dust.

The brass plate at the bottom of the portrait

Eugene William Bohannon
President, Duluth State Teachers College
1901–1938

is a small grave marker in a toy cemetery,
a headstone at the foot of a canvas imitation
of life forgotten for a half-century
while the world beyond the storage vault
reinvented itself history repeating history,
the robed and seated scholar shrouded
indefinitely in brown paper secured by twine
while he waited as Wells's time traveler
for the machine to halt and tip him sideways
back into the endless argument over what is light
and what is dark, what is Eloi and what is Morlock.

Since his resurrection, E.W. has seen the light
of day only in the building that bears his name
in this dreamlike portrait painted
in what looks like the most civilized of times.
From behind glass he blinks, slowly,
through the reflection of my grandmother's eyes
at this loiterer that I am,
who pauses more often than she should at this case
to wonder, to ponder the parallel worlds
between his existence, her grandmother's, and her own,
attempting and failing to reconcile the present with the past.

Fearlessly—I hope—we stare him down,
my grandmother's shadow and I.
Without expression we blink slowly back
at E. W. Bohannon, upright under glass.

Migwechiwendam Ojibwemowin

O'o apii ninganawaamabamaag noozhishenyag,
ingiw minawaanagwe'odeg,
nimiigwechiwendam.

Onaangi wii'awensiwaan
gaye ozide'iwaan naanimiwag
amanj igo api mawadeshiwewaad
omishomisimiwaa gaye ookomisimiwaa owaakaa'iganiwag.
Ninzaagitoon oninjiwan
iniw oninjiiniwaan nimbi-biidamawigoog
wenizhishid asin
misko'ode ziizibaakwadoonsan
gikinjigwewin
zoomiingweniwin gaye bozagozid ojiimewin.

Ninzhawendaagoz.

Ayaangodinong nimaaminowendam komisag.
Mewinsha giigoi ishpiming
nasaab noongoom megwe'oog niinawin.
O'o apii ninganawaabamaag noozhishenyag
nimaaminonendaanan gete gizhigoon gaye awas-waabang,
mii dash ningikwendam
ninzhaawendaagoz ikweyaan, niin.

Mi dash ni migwechiwendam.

Migwech, dash minawaa migwech.

Migwechiwendam Shaaganashiimowin

When I look at my grandchildren
those sweet and happy hearts,
I think with gratitude.

Their bodies are small and light,
and their little feet dance
when they visit
at their grandpa's and grandma's house.
I love their small hands
that bring to me
a pretty rock
red heart candy
a hug
a smile and a sticky kiss.

I am fortunate.

Sometimes
I think about my grandmothers.
A long time ago they went to live in heaven,
yet they are still at this same time with us.
When I look at my grandchildren
I consider the old days and the present,
today and tomorrow and the day after tomorrow,
and then I know
that I am blessed, a fortunate woman.

And I think with gratitude.

Migwech, and again migwech.

Niizhwaasimidana

in honor of Joy Harjo's "Becoming Seventy"

_____

My father said to me
the most important word to know is migwech
when you get up in the morning
you should thank God for making you an Indian

at seventy I remember what he said
he never spoke without first giving thought

but at seventy I cannot remember
the times and places, where he said this, and when

was it driving west in his green truck at sunset
late winter giizis orange against purple clouds;
or waiting inside the entryway of the public library
for the rain to let up—back home, the roof held
where he and Uncle Ray had fixed the biggest leak,
the boards covering where Ray's leg had dropped
through rotting wood miraculously dry

or after an auntie's funeral
Carol, her hair perfect as always
in her good sweater with the sequins,
or Jessie queenly in her blue peignoir set
bought especially for the occasion

or after a birth, new life in the world
or a Rosemary Clooney song playing on the radio

or handing us kids his lunchbox after work,
watching us eat what he had saved—

the end of a candy bar, two or three grapes,
part of a scrambled egg and ketchup sandwich

what I have learned at seventy is this,
that the time and place are not as important
as what he said, the words my father spoke
that had become a prayer without ceasing

the most important word to know is migwech
when you get up in the morning
you should thank God for making you an Indian

Migwech

I would like to thank Susan Gardner and Devon Ross of Red Mountain Press for their publication of the poems in the 2016 edition of *The Sky Watched,* and Denise Low for her initial reading of the manuscript; the wonderful people at the University of Minnesota Press for this new and expanded edition; and the many people in this world and the next who are part of this collection and who continue to be of such inspiration.

How can I express my appreciation, my admiration, and my gratitude? As the old Ojibweg say, *migwech* is enough.

Migwech.

Publication History

"Redemption" from *The Cambridge History of American Poetry,* A. Bendison and S. Burt, editors (New York: Cambridge University Press, 2014).

"Sea Smoke on Gichigami" from *Gichigami Hearts: Stories and Histories from Misaabekong* (Minneapolis: University of Minnesota Press, 2021).

"Everything You Need to Know in Life You'll Learn at Boarding School" from *When the Light of the World Was Subdued, Our Songs Came Through: A Norton Anthology of Native Nations Poetry,* J. Harjo, L. Howe, and J. E. Foerster, editors (New York: W. W. Norton, 2020).

"Everything You Need to Know in Life You'll Learn at Boarding School," "South Dakota Mission School, 1890," "Leaving," "Ma at Home," "Bemidji," "Grandmother at Indian School," "Lights Out" (here titled "The Canticle of the Night"), "Lugalette," "Bernadette," "Bruneaux," "Mary Remembering on a July Afternoon," "Order," "Town, As I Recall It," "Escape," "Chi Ko-ko-koho and the Boarding School Prefect, 1934," "Miss Shawn," "For Asin," "The Class of 1968," "To the Woman Who Just Bought a Set of Native American Spirituality Dream Interpretation Cards," "Mary Susan," and "The Refugees" from *THE.INDIAN.AT.INDIAN.SCHOOL* (Little Rock: University of Arkansas, 2009).

"Ma at Home," "Everything You Need to Know in Life You'll Learn at Boarding School," and "Leaving" from *North Coast Review* 22 (2003).

"Grandmother at Indian School," "St. Bernard," "Everything You Need to Know in Life You'll Learn at Boarding School," "To the Woman Who Just Bought That Set of Native American Spirituality Dream Interpretion Cards," "Nindaaniss Waawaashkeshiikwesens on a Winter Night," "Chi Ko-ko-koho and the Boarding School Prefect," "Redemption," and "The Refugees" from *Traces in Blood, Bone, and Stone: Contemporary Ojibwe Poetry* (Loonfeather Press, 2006).

"The Refugees" from *phati'tude Literary Magazine* (November 2001).

"The Beanbag," "Winona Conceives the Trickster," and "Parturition" from *Yellow Medicine Review: A Journal of Indigenous Literature, Art, and Thought* (Marshall, Minn.: Southwest Minnesota State University, Winter 2007).

"Lost and Astigmatic Twenty-Nine-Year-Old Self" from *Yellow Medicine Review: A Journal of Indigenous Literature, Art, and Thought* (Marshall, Minn.: Southwest Minnesota State University, Fall 2015).

"The Girls of Casualty Days" from *The Roaring Muse* (Duluth: Department of English, University of Minnesota Duluth, Spring 2001).

"Parturition: A Poem for Brenda" and "The Beanbag" from *Migrations: Prose and Poetry for Life's Transitions* (Duluth, Minn.: Wildwood Press, 2011).

"To the Woman Who Just Bought That Set of Native American Spirituality Dream Interpretation Cards," "Ikwe Ishpiming," and "Chi Ko-ko-koho and the Boarding School Prefect" from *Sister Nations* (St. Paul: Minnesota Historical Society Press, 2009).

"Nindaaniss Waawasshkeshiikwesens on a Winter Night" and "My Dad, Who Treats Life like a Sacrament" from *My Home As I Remember* (Natural Heritage Books, 2000).

"Nindaaniss Waawaashkeshiikwesens on a Winter Night" and "Redemption" from *Trail Guide to the Northland Experience in Prints and Poetry* (Corvallis, Ore.: Calyx Press, 2008).

"Anishinaabikwe-Everywoman" from *Dust & Fire* (Bemidji, Minn.: Bemidji State University, 2007).

"Migwechiwendam Shaaganaashiimowin" and "Redemption" from *Flight Scape: A Multi-Directional Collection of Indigenous Writings* (Penticton, B.C.: Theytus Books, 2001).

Linda LeGarde Grover is professor emerita of American Indian studies at the University of Minnesota Duluth and a member of the Bois Forte Band of Ojibwe. She is the author of *Onigamiising: Seasons of an Ojibwe Year* and *Gichigami Hearts: Stories and Histories from Misaabekong* and the novels *The Road Back to Sweetgrass* and *In the Night of Memory,* all published by the University of Minnesota Press. Her short fiction collection *The Dance Boots* received the Flannery O'Connor Award for Short Fiction and the Janet Heidinger Kafka Prize.